A Beginner's Guide to Sailing

By Doug Werner

Published By

Publishing

San Diego, California

Sailor's Start-Up:
A Beginner's Guide to Sailing
By Doug Werner

Tracks Publishing
140 Brightwood Avenue
Chula Vista, CA 91910
(619) 476-7125

Copyright©1994 by Doug Werner
Second Printing 1994
Third Printing 1997

Publisher's Cataloging in Publication
(Prepared by Quality Books Inc.)

Werner, Doug.   1950-
  Sailor's start-up : a beginner's guide to sailing / by
Doug Werner.
  p. cm. – (Start-up sports ; #3)
  Includes bibliographical references and index.
  Preassigned LCCN: 93-94343
  ISBN: 1-884654-03-7

  1. Sailing.   I. Title. II. Series.

GV811 .W47 1994   797.1'24
                                   QBI93-22653

To

ANN WERNER

and

EUGENE WERNER

for your
50th Anniversary
1-29-94

ACKNOWLEDGMENTS

Kathleen Wheeler (always!)
Rich Gleason
Dee Gleason
Cliff Graves
Connie Max
Jason Boone
Ron Lane
Debbie Lane
Karen Driscoll
Craig McClain
Leah Malloy
Eugene Wheeler
Eugenie Wheeler
Bruce Richards
John Beazley
Tom Heasley
Image & Form Design Consultants
Catalina Yachts
Charles L. Nichols

PREFACE

I didn't read any of the hundreds of how-to sailing books available as I put this ditty together. I wanted *Sailor's Start-Up* to be a stew of individual experiences together with the supreme expertise of my able friends at the Mission Bay Sportcenter (MBSC) here in San Diego, California.

I wanted to avoid the textbook approach that plagues this and many other sports. The MBSC method and mine are one and the same: DO IT and DO IT FUN! Learning how to sail should be a good time out in the WATER. Not in a classroom or milling around on the dock.

I also wanted to have fun writing it. So besides the how-to stuff there are anecdotes, a yarn or two, and in general, a light-heartedness throughout. The world doesn't need another picky instructional handbook. Especially about sailing.

Actually, what the beginner in any endeavor needs is a friendly hand. Just a few pointers and a pat on the back. There's plenty of time later to be demanding.

MANY THANKS to the special folks at the MBSC for making this project such a treat. And for enduring it all with smiles intact.

Doug Werner

CONTENTS

— INTRODUCTION —
GET OUT THERE!

Philosophy

Sailing is many, many things. It's a hobby. It's a sport. It's an intellectual pursuit. It's a passion. It's a social thing. It's an individual thing. It's complicated. It's simple. It's relaxing. It's exciting. It's a labor. It's a labor of love. It's poetic, popular, yet vaguely elitist. It's ancient, eternal and silly in some ways. But front page, futuristic and hip as well.

I think it's FUN.

And that's my philosophy about sailing. Doing it. Learning it. Teaching it. Writing it. It's gotta be fun first.

The Goal

Get out in the water.

The sooner that happens, the sooner the fun starts. And the learning.

This book's about what you need to know to get started with this sailing stuff. It's simple and straightforward. No long diatribes about theory. No baffling passages of nautical jargon and strategies. No long-winded explanations of why, what, and how. Just what you need to know. To sail fun and safe ASAP.

The Method

If you have never sailed, these questions are pop-popping in your head, or should be.

1) What do I wear?

2) What do I sail in?

3) What are the parts of the boat I need to know now?

4) Where do I sail?

5) When do I sail?

6) How do I set up the boat?

7) How do I leave the dock?

8) How do I make it go this way and that way?

9) How do I get back?

10) Where are the brakes?

Ten simple questions. Notice none of the words have more than 6 letters. Simple questions deserve simple answers. If the philosophy is to have fun, and the goal is to get out in the water right away--the method had better be simple or you'll get hung up in the classroom. Or worse, reading this book.

Instruction

Get some.

This book will whet your appetite, get you STARTED, and become a RESOURCE as you fumble about during your first few days.

But real-live instruction is practically irreplaceable. A good teacher has a much better chance to impart knowledge, inspire confidence, and imprint the sailing experience than mere words on paper.

Now. You can learn from a friend or relative but it could very well destroy the friendship or the family tie. Strange things happen between intimate folks when one or the other becomes 'Coach'. Just 'cause someone's a great mom or dad or chum or mate and a good sailor does not mean he\she will be a good instructor.

Rent a professional. They've done it before. A thousand times. They know how to do it right and they know how to deal with yearlings like you. Any place that has sailing has instruction, somewhere. Ask around and shop around. It'll be a good investment (although it shouldn't cost that much), and an education (one in which you'll actually learn something).

It's an opportunity to rub shoulders with authentic sailing people in their natural habitat and to learn with other learners like you. (Take a class. They're cheaper than private lessons and there's bound to be someone more inept than you to laugh at.)

So why the book? Even the best instruction may not cover things adequately for you. You'll forget things and\or remain confused about this or that. Instruction also comes and goes. The book is a handy-dandy reference that'll stick around for awhile, and makes an excellent coffee table coaster when you're through with it.

1

WHAT TO WEAR

The boat you SHOULD be in will not (well, shouldn't) tip over. So you needn't worry about getting wet. Dress like you would if you were just strolling the water's edge. Warm enough or cool enough so that you're comfortable.

From head to toe:

➤ *Hat with visor or brim*
   The sun is bad news and that's not trendy advice. If you're thinning on top, caps are a must (baldy burns). Make sure it stays on your noggin.

➤ *Sunglasses*
   The glare off the water is...glaring. Unless you enjoy viewing the waterscape in a white-out with a headache, wear eye protection. With a strap.

➤ **Sunscreen**
   For all exposed body parts. Skin cancer is a clear and present danger to all outdoor folks. Use it.

➤ **Sneakers**
   With light-colored soles. You'll be scrambling about in the boat so something with a grip is required.

➤ **Life preservers**
   This is the law. One for each sailor. Not necessarily worn but in the boat.

Now as you progress and try tippier boats you will dump. And you'll need to consider wetsuits or drysuits in cooler water and/or weather. But that's later.

White Gloves or
Good Things Happen to Sailors

My wife grew up in Antigua, your typical Caribbean island paradise. Naturally, besides climbing coconut trees, she sailed a lot. On her daddy's 33' cutter and all by herself, on her 10', single-sail Sunfish.

One fine day Kathleen was zipping about on her little boat, when she passed one of the large yachts that periodically anchored in the historic harbor. Antigua was and still is a favorite destination for sailors the world over.

This particular yacht, as everyone on the island knew, belonged to a certain Lady (yes, that's lady with a capital 'L'). At the time, our Lady was one of the wealthiest women on the globe due to several profitable marriage ventures. A real jet setter before the age of jets (plane person?), she was pretty much a Jackie O type, what with her royal pals, mansions, globe trotting and, of course, her yachts.

Chapter One

In Step! In Style! — *Cliff and Connie show off their sailing duds -*
sneakers, shorts and shades.

A Jackie O, that is, with sass. For example, the Lady wore a gold leotard and arm length white gloves... waterskiing. She liked to ski with two boats. One that pulled and one that followed closely. No doubt with dry gloves. And quite unlike our American icon, she was not afraid to show her teeth. When she didn't receive an invitation to Grace Kelly's marriage to the Prince of Monaco, she tore the Monacan flag to shreds in public view.

Yes sir! She was quite a gal. I picture this Kate Hepburn type with fire in her eyes and an arrogance so outlandish that it becomes endearing. Even admirable. My kinda dame!

Anyway, on this particular day, as Kathleen sailed by this big ol' yacht, the Lady spied this rare child sailor and had one of the crew call her over. Kathleen docked herself next to the yacht and was escorted to an upper deck where the Lady was entertaining a dozen guests. Actually they were eating lunch, if you can call 12 courses, white linen, crystal, waiters, et al, 'lunch'. She was seated next to some countess and proceeded to spend the afternoon wining and dining with the kind of folks most of us read about in the tabloids.

Kathleen was such a hit that the Lady wanted to take her away on a world cruise. Kathleen declined, however, explaining that her Daddy needed her help scraping the barnacles off the bottom of his boat. So she and the Lady bade each other adieu, all the rich people smiled, waved bye-bye, and Kathleen sailed back home.

Now this story illustrates one point and explains another. That good things happen to sailors. We just sail under a lucky star.

And it explains why my wife insists on sailing with arm length white gloves. (Just kidding.)

2

THE RIGHT BOAT

One of the major factors involved in happy beginnings.

Sailboats are like cars, computers, and portable heaters. There are a billion makes and models. What makes sailboats different is that they've had another 2000 years or so to refine the confusion. Yes, the world of sailing LOVES to baffle the uninitiated. Wait'll you see the glossary!

But the right boat for you is easy to describe and easy to find. I would suggest a 14' monohull. Monohull means one hull. As opposed to two, like a catamaran. It's a model that's available most places that have sailing. They are built by several different manufacturers the world over.

These boats are big enough for up to four people, yet quite manageable for one. The common version is wide and steady (it won't capsize easily), simple to rig, and easy to handle. They're also relatively inexpensive

The Right Boat — *A 14' monohull. Not too big, not too small.*

and reliable (they last forever). In short, they're a good, basic sailboat for beginning, intermediate, and just plain fun, cruise-around sailing.

Stay away from anything much bigger. There's usually more stuff to confuse. And they can be intimidating. It's more comfortable to feel out of control on a 14' boat than a 22' boat. (What?) There's more boat to crash. (Oh.)

Smaller boats are OK but avoid the tippy ones. Certain models may seem dorky and\or too cramped for adults. You want something that's comfy enough to spend some time in, steady enough that you can concentrate on your sailing, and dry enough that you don't have to worry about getting wet. Of course, if the water is 80 degrees and the air temp is 80 degrees, getting damp is hardly a problem.

Learn the basics in a monohull. Catamarans are sexy but a bit tricky. Learn how to walk, then you can fly.

Mind you that this is a vast simplification of what's what in sailboats. But simple is what you need for now. Trust me.

Where's the Boat?

Find a place that RENTS. That way all you have to do is show up in your yachting ensemble. No trailers, no ramps, no parking your boat in the alley, etc., etc. Buy later when you know something and you're sure you want to try backing boat and trailer into the garage.

The Right Boat

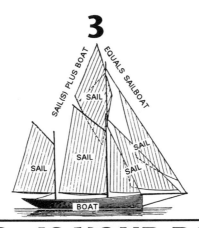

3

THIS...IS YOUR BOAT
OR PARTS IS PARTS

Sailboats are simple once you get down to basics (and keep it there!)

Sails

Every sailboat has at least one sail. (Absolutely true.) Our boat has two. A big one called a main sail, and a little one called a jib. A boat with this configuration is called a sloop. The way sails work is really very interesting, but now is not the time. I'll get into theory later.

Why two sails? Because more sail means more area for the wind which means faster sailing. You don't need two sails. Just make sure you have one.

Mast

And every sailboat has one of these. It holds up the sails.

Boom

This is the wooden or metal beam attached to the mast and the bottom of the main sail. It stabilizes the sail. It's called a boom because it swings back and forth when you turn. If it hits you, it go boom.

Sheets

No. Not the billowy part of the sails. Strangely enough, this is the name for the ropes attached to the sails. The sheets allow you to adjust the tension in the sails, which in turn helps adjust the speed of your boat. The main sheet sprouts from a swivel gizmo (cleat) in the middle\bottom of the hull. The jib has two, angling in from cleats on either side of the boat.

Cleats

The gizmos that tie down the sheets have teeth that always let you pull in. The teeth prevent the sails from pulling out. A yank up or down frees the sheet. A yank the other way sets the teeth.

Daggerboard/Centerboard

This is the thing jutting out from underneath the boat. If it pops in and out, it's called a daggerboard. If it pivots, it's called a centerboard. Both serve the same functions. They stabilize the craft and play a major role in the physics of sailing. More on that later. For now, just remember you need one or the other.

Chapter Three

Boat Parts — *Most of what you need to know.*

Slipping in the daggerboard.

Jib cleat and sheet. The main cleat works about the same only it swivels.

Starboard (right) and port (left) as you face forward towards the bow.

Yikes! Ropes and wires everywhere!

Tiller and Rudder

The tiller is your steering wheel and the rudder is your tires. You hold on to the tiller which is attached to the rudder. The rudder is the part in the water. Push or pull one way and you turn in the opposite direction. Don't even try to visualize it. Once you get out there it'll come together without much thought.

Hull

The boat part of the boat.

Luff

Believe it or not, there are up to a dozen parts to a sail. For now just commit this to memory. The luff is the leading edge of the jib and main sails. The luff indicates sail tension.

Telltails

Telltails are strips of fabric attached to the sails or to the shrouds on either side of the boat. They indicate wind direction. Shrouds are the wires that hold up the mast.

Bow

The front of the boat.

Stern

The back of the boat.

Port

As you face forward inside your boat, this is the left side.

Starboard

The right side.

You know, even if somone had an explanation for these last two terms (I refuse to research it) there is no, repeat no, defense for the use of these words. I can think of no other human endeavor that deliberately confuses the left and right. It's reprehensable. Right up there with green pasta, detergent commercials, and California's incomprehensible sales taxes.

No Sheet

"Grab the sheet!" he shouted as our boat headed into the first leg of the race.

I was along for 'fun,' in a 'fun' race, although I knew nothing about sailing and less about sailing terminology, as I was about to prove. We were tacking around the first marker and the boom had just swung around. Sails were a flappin' and ropes were every-which-way, as is the case before you set the sails.

It was my job to man the jib. Easy enough, really. Just uncleat the rope on one side of the boat and cleat the rope on the other side when the boat turns, or tacks, and the boom swoops around. That's what I was about to do when the skipper bellowed instructions about this 'sheet.'

"The sheet! Grab the sheet! Pull in the sheet NOW!" he barked.

Not wanting to hesitate in the thick of it, I went after what had to be the sheet. Sheets are either fabric or paper, right? I mean that's how it comes. In sheets. The only thing close to that were the sails. Sheets. Sails. That's gotta be it!

So I leapt up onto the bow and wrassled with my jib. "Got it! Now what?!" I yelled as I stumbled and grasped.

"Hey, whattya doing!" Mr. Skip answered in a not so pleasant way. "Get down here and pull in the sheet!"

Somewhat dismayed and confused, I managed to regain my seat in the hull. "What's a sheet?" I asked.

"The rope! This rope!" he exclaimed grabbing one of the ropes attached to the jib and cleating it down. The same job I was about to do before all this sheet stuff started.

Well, of course. A sheet is a rope. How stupid of me.

By this time we're totally out of it. All the loose sheets, my dance on the bow and my verbal ineptitude had cost us the race. We came in dead last. As we approached the dock, the cat calls began. It was ugly.

I thought it was funny, but Captain Ahab didn't. He proceeded to explain things to me in a faintly authoritarian manner (this is a symptom of a common personality disfunction associated with sailing that will be explored later). As if any sort of explanation could excuse calling a rope a sheet.

That was my first experience with THE CODE.

Get used to it, folks. 'Cause that's sailing. Although I work around it here in order to make things simple, beware that in the strange, yet real world of docks, marinas and clubs, the names for things don't make sense. It's all a part of an ancient conspiracy of sailors the world over.

But more on that later.

Parts is Parts

4

CONDITIONS

You gotta have the right boat, and you gotta have the right conditions to learn in. The boat you know about...

Water

You can sail on lakes, rivers, bays, and oceans. The common denominator is water. The place you learn should be deep enough to allow for your daggerboard or centerboard. (Oh, really?). Yes. Really. Every year even the old salts find themselves high and dry because they didn't know the bottom. (Does the name 'Valdez' ring any bells?) Know where the sandbars, reefs, sunken wrecks, and ancient cities are located before you cast off.

And pick a place that isn't swarming with traffic. You're going to be sailing wild and loose for awhile, so make sure you have room to be a kook.

Conditions

A great place to start. Moderate wind. No boats!

If you see 'em doing this (flying a hull) it's probably too windy for comfy learning.

Chapter Four

As a rule, a good place to begin is a small, enclosed bay or cove off a larger body of water. Winds are usually lighter in such places than over an open expanse. There you're probably not dealing with waves, shipping lanes, dangerous currents, 18 foot sharks, or pirates, either.

Wind

Look at the other sailboats already out and about. How are they moving along? If their hulls are flying (lifting out of the water), the wind is too much for you now. If the boats are sailing at a moderate pace, go for it. A very light wind is fine. Just make sure the sailors and their vessels are moving.

No boats? Check out the chop. If it's whitecapping, the wind is at least 12 knots and too strong. The higher the chop, the greater the wind. Flags can help, of course. An expert opinion at this point is a good idea. The thing is, you don't want to learn in difficult conditions. I know this sounds a tad vague, but like everything else in sailing, you'll get a better feel for things as you progress. Right now it's easy does it. Mild winds with just enough push in a safe, secluded patch of wa-wa.

Conditions

5

A LITTLE CLASSWORK

You don't learn it until your doin' it, but there is a bit of lore you need to know before you set out. Sailing is all about wind. Wind determines all your moves. After all, you will be riding IT...

The Wind Pie *(See diagram 5a)*

This doesn't look like fun. Here you thought you'd be reading about billowing sails and spray-in-yer-face, and I give you this. Something out of high school geometry. Bear with me.

You can't sail directly into the wind (UPWIND). In fact, you can't sail under 45 degrees to either side. This is called the DEAD ZONE. If you're pointed into the dead zone, you stop. Dead.

Despite its name, the dead zone is very important and useful when you turn and dock the boat. It's also

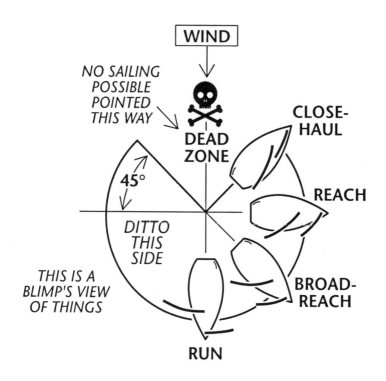

WIND

NO SAILING
POSSIBLE
POINTED
THIS WAY

DEAD
ZONE

CLOSE-
HAUL

45°

REACH

DITTO
THIS
SIDE

THIS IS A
BLIMP'S VIEW
OF THINGS

BROAD-
REACH

RUN

DIAGRAM 5A

The Wind Pie — *Indicated are the directions you can sail and their proper names. These are called points of sail. The left side is the same as the right. All direction is determined by wind source. (It all makes perfect sense in the water.)*

Chapter Five

Tacking — *From the wind pie you take a zigzag course that is comprised of close-hauled courses and 90 degree, upwind turns (tacks). The zigs and zags are necessary in order to sail around the dead zone. This is the only way to reach an upwind bearing in a sailboat.*

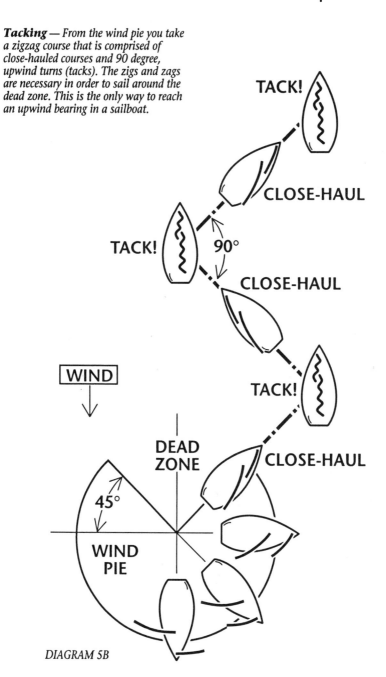

TACK!

CLOSE-HAUL

TACK!

90°

CLOSE-HAUL

WIND

TACK!

CLOSE-HAUL

DEAD ZONE

45°

WIND PIE

DIAGRAM 5B

a good place to be pointed when your in trouble, or just confused. Because you...stop! It's always nice to know where the brakes are.

Everywhere else on the pie you'll move. CLOSE-HAULED is as close to upwind that you can travel.

REACHING is sailing 90 degrees to wind direction.

RUNNING is sailing with the wind (downwind).

BROAD-REACHING is sailing in-between reaching and running. All these directions are called POINTS OF SAIL.

Tacking *(See diagram 5b)*

This is awful, isn't it? But get a grip. This is the hardest part.

It's easy to go left and right and down.

The stickler is going up, as in upwind. Somehow you have to zig and zag around the dead zone. All this zigging and zagging is called TACKING. It looks like turning...and that's what it is.

The trick to tacking involves switching the sides that you and the sails have been operating.

Okie Doke. All done for now. Let's go sailing.

6

HEADING OUT!

Leaving the Dock

First things first. Which way is the wind blowing? Remember your wind pie. You cannot sail into the wind or less than 45 degrees to either side. So make sure the wind is coming from the side or from behind your boat. If it isn't, you must walk, paddle or tow your boat into such a position so that it is. Make sure the direction you're headed is open water and clear sailing.

Determine which side of the boat the main sail and its boom will be before you board. Unless you're pointed upwind, the main sail will want to be on one side or the other. You don't have to force the issue.

Ready? A bunch of things should happen at once if you're doing this alone. Of course, if you have some

Shoving Off — *Cliff holds the boat steady while Tom settles in at the tiller. The boat is positioned so that the wind will take it towards open water.*

Cliff steps into the center of the boat next to the mast. At the same time he pushes off the dock with the other foot.

As Cliff settles in, Tom steers the boat into open water...

... and pulls in the main sheet in order to adjust the main sail.

Chapter Six

Cliff reaches for the jib sheet in order to adjust the jib sail.

Note that Tom is always looking ahead, always has a hand on the tiller, and always has hold of the main sheet.

Trimming adjustments are made on jib and main sails. Both Cliff and Tom will seek to make taut foils of their sails.

The way is clear, and away they go.

help pushing off you can settle in first. And if you have a companion you can split the chores.

Untie the boat and push off the dock with one foot, as you step towards the center of the boat, next to the mast, with the other.

Settle in next to the tiller opposite the sail and grab hold of the tiller and the main sheet. Pull the main sheet in just enough to get going. As the sail fills, steer clear of the docking area. Pick a point on the opposite shore and aim for it. This is setting a bearing.

By now the jib is flapping (luffing), so pull it in with the jib sheet on the same side as the main sail and cleat it down.

If you've been counting, in the span of five seconds or so you have been asked to grapple with three things (tiller, main sheet and jib sheet) with only two hands. Pretty tricky, huh? Not to mention the scrambling around and the guy on the dock shouting at you incoherently.

Now is an excellent time to panic, but don't. If you must, let the jib flap away for a bit and just concentrate on handling the mainsail and steering out to open water. Do set it, though, as soon as you can.

All the juggling becomes more and more manageable as you clock in more and more sailing time. Look. This part is just sorta complicated and fumbling at first. Like driving a stick shift or sliding on skis or swinging a golf club. Hey. You're a kook. Relax and go with the flow. Don't get mad or embarrassed or frazzled. You will get it eventually.

Just stay away from everybody and everything until you do!

OK. Back to your initial trim.

Trimming

Trimming your sails is all about pulling in on your sheets until the sails stop flapping. What you want are nice taut foils of sail. This tautness indicates proper sail tension. The first and last part of the sails to flap are the luffs or leading edges of both jib and main sails. Hence the luffs are terrific check points for adjusting sail tension and trim.

When in doubt--let 'em out!

To find proper sail trim at any point after you've set a bearing, let your sails out until they flap or luff. (Yes, the word 'luff' can be a subject or a verb. And sometimes at the same time.) Then pull 'em in until you got those full, wrinkle-free foils. The look and feel of properly trimmed sails is something you'll pick up fairly quickly with practice, and is definitely one of the major sweetspots in sailing.

So you've pulled in your jib and cleated it down. And you've pulled in your main sail. Don't cleat this one because trimming is a constant thing. At this point you're holding the main sheet with one hand and the tiller with the other-- steering towards the bearing you set earlier. And that's your sailor's 'stance'. One hand monitors the sail and one hand steers the boat. You've got an eye on your sails and the water all around you....All the time.

Well whaddaya know! You're SAILING. Just scooting along without gas fumes, noise or traffic lights. And NO BOOM BOXES. Pretty neat, huh? Just like Jimmy Buffett, John Paul Jones, and Chris Columbus.

By now you've discovered why you sit where you do. The sail wants to pull one way, and your sitting on the opposite side balances things out. This is trimming the boat itself. Of course the other reason for sitting there is to SEE. The sail's in yer face otherwise.

Scoot up or back to achieve the proper trim fore (front) and aft (back). You want the boat to cut level through the water. Not bow up or down.

7

ON A REACH

OK. Let's discover the reality of the Wind Pie. Actually, at this point you've already found out about a piece of it, since you've probably been on a reach or thereabouts since you left the dock. A reach is sailing at right angles to the wind. That's probably your position because that's the optimum direction for sail and boat trim, as well as speed. It's like the natural notch to slide into. The telltails on your shrouds should be streaming at a 90 degree angle to the length of the boat.

Stay on this course for awhile. Get a feel for the lift of the boat, the tug of the sheet and sail, and the tiller in your hand. Sailing is all about balancing those things and it really does boil down to feel. There's no computerized gizmo to guide you, and who would want it! Half the charge of sailing is seeking the forces that move you and tapping into their energy.

So dial into the lifts and tugs. Notice they change.

That's because the wind isn't a constant. It usually blows in gusts. On the same heading or bearing you'll constantly adjust sail tension. Puffs of wind will hit and away you'll go. Sometimes so hard the sail will pull your boat over. In that case, let out the sail. On a reach you pull in to gain speed and let out to slow down. Turn the boat towards the dead zone (upwind) if need be. That'll settle things down.

Conversely, in order to speed up, reel in your sheets and make sure your telltails are sideways into the sail.

Why does the boat speed so on a reach? Why does pulling in or letting out the sail make the boat go fast and slow? An explanation requires some theoretical song and dance, and now ain't showtime. There's a chapter on that stuff later.

Capsized!

One of these days you're gonna capsize. It happens to everybody who sails small boats. It has always happened to me on a reach. When I've set my sails too tight and the wind just blew me over.

Getting upright is usually no big deal.

Normally when a sailboat capsizes, it's lying on its side with the mast and sails floating on top of the water. After you've resurfaced from your dunking, swim over to the boat and uncleat the sheets. You don't want the sails to act as buckets when you rock the boat upright. Also, a boat with sheets cleated will take off as soon as it's erect. This is important because chances are you won't be in the boat yet. (Hey! Stop that boat!)

On a Reach — *The wind is blowing straight into Cliff's back— 90 degrees to the length of the boat. Sails are about halfway out. Note the full foil shape of these trimmed sails.*

Capsize Recovery — The first thing Cliff did was release the sails. Otherwise, they'd act as buckets and he'd never pull the boat over.

Cliff grabs hold of the centerboard and pulls down.

Tom comes over to help.

Come on guys . . .

Chapter Seven

What's the problem?

There you go! The sails have popped free of the water.

And voila!

Up 'n' at 'em. It should be noted that capsizing doesn't happen very often in these boats. It took longer to tip it over than it did to right it.

Paddle over to the centerboard which should be sticking out like a platform. Scramble up on it and grab on to the side of the boat. As you stand up the boat should right itself without much fuss. Unless, of course, something bizarre is underfoot...

The Mast-in-Mud Incident

As is the normal course of events for calamity, this mishap occurred when I was trying to impress someone. It was my date's first time on a sailboat and I was going to teach her how to sail. This, by the way, is a tried and true mating ritual wherever sails are unfurled. It goes something like this...

"Hello, There".

"Well, hello yourself, big boy".

"Wanna see my sailboat?"

"I'm with you Mr. Skipperman!"

Works every time.

So off we went in my boat. It was cozy 'cause we were in an itty-bitty Laser. Lasers are squirrelly, zippy, and tippy. A real blast if you don't mind getting wet. We zoomed along for awhile in a moderate wind, just having a high ol' time.

Now Lasers like to pop their hulls way up out of the water when a gust hits on a reach. What you do then is hook your feet underneath the hiking strap in the cockpit and lean out over the water in order to compensate for the sail, which is pulling the other way.

It can be a real bronco ride and successfully executing those hikes can really impress a pretty passenger.

Until you dump.

Like I said, Lasers are tippy and capsizing is part of the game when you max out on a reach. But, hey. So we got a little wet. No harm done. The water was warm, we were in our suits, and flipping the thing upright would be a snap. Just uncleat the sheet, stand on the centerboard, and presto! We'd be back in business.

My date looked a little nervous treading water out there, in the middle of the bay, but I assured her and swam over to the boat to right it.

Something, however, was odd. Usually when you dump, the boat floats sideways on the water. The sail lays flat on the water, preventing the boat from turning all the way over. Yet this time the center board was thrusting straight up. The sail was nowhere to be seen. My little boat was completely upside down.

What a pickle.

Trying not to display the concern that was welling in my mind, I reached up, got a grip on my centerboard and tried to yank my ship over.

Not a budge.

I planted my feet on the hull and tried again.

Nada.

Glancing at my crew, I noticed that her nervous look had changed to a squinty grimace that typically indicates the onset of *ohmygodwhatarewegonnadonow* syndrome.

This was grim. My manhood was at stake! It was time for assertion. Action. Heroics, even.

So I dove. Straight down along the mast to discover that its tip was buried in a foot of mud. I resurfaced after a bit of digging to report back and catch a breath.

She stared wide-eyed at my muddiness extremus and no doubt heard none of my reassurances... "It's OK. All I have to do is dig the mast out of the bottom of the bay".

She said nothing. She just hung on the hull like the victim she'd become. She was either in shock or too mad to speak.

I returned to my buried mast and this time managed to free it. I pushed it back to the surface, hopped back onto the centerboard, and with a grunt, hauled the sucker up and over. We pulled ourselves back into the boat, I reset the sail, and away we putted.

My date? Well, she lost her evil-eye, heaved an unmistakable sigh of relief, and gave me an oh-my-hero look. She sat very close and patted my leg.

Hmmmmm. Not bad. The old rescue-the-damsel-in-distress routine. (Never mind that I provided the distress.)

Works every time.

DOWNWIND SAILING

Sailing with the wind (downwind) is perhaps the easiest direction to maintain in light to moderate wind. Oddly enough it's just about the slowest way to go, and since you set your sail just one way when you travel downwind, there's next to zero adjustments to make along the way.

Turn downwind and let out your sails. All the way. Your telltails should be streaming straight ahead. Adjust the main sail so that it sticks out at a 90 degree to the boat. Chances are your jib won't even work because the main sail is in the way. You can try sheeting the jib on the opposite side to the main, but it may or may not do much. Hold it right there and whistle a tune. Das all dey is to it.

You're wondering how come a sailboat sails so slow going with the wind, right? It seems that it ought to be the swiftest path. Again, the reason is slightly technical and I don't wanna deal with it here. I will dog it out later, however.

Downwind Sailing

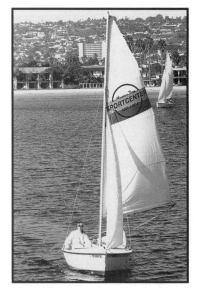

Running — *The wind is blowing directly over the stern of the boat. The sails are adjusted all the way out. In the first pix, the jib and main sails are set on opposite sides in order achieve maximum use of both sails. However (as is often the case), the jib fizzles out after a short spell and only the main remains.*

Jibing *(See diagram 8a)*

A faster way to travel downwind involves sailing in a series of zigzags towards your downwind bearing. Although this course is longer, since you're angling downwind on a broad-reach, it's faster than sailing directly downwind.

As you can see, this zigzagging requires changing direction or turning at certain intervals. The turn used in downwind sailing is called a jibe. Simply put, jibing is pulling the tiller towards you.

Jibes are a little tricky because the sails catch the wind so quickly as you turn. The boom swings around fast and can catch you unprepared. In a strong wind, a jibe can really jolt both you and the boat. Not a good thing.

1) Before you do anything, look in the direction you want to go and make sure the way is clear.

2) Make sure you're pointed on a broad-reach. NEVER JIBE FROM A REACH. You do not want to go into a jibe with too much speed.

3) Pull the tiller towards you...

4) Release both sails (uncleat jib and main sails)...

5) Switch sides and DUCK as the boom swings around...

6) Set your sails (cleat jib and haul in main)...

7) Find your broad-reach course and get a bearing on the shore.

With practice, you'll get a feel for this maneuver and the rhythm of sailing on a broad-reach, making a jibe, sailing on a broad-reach, making a jibe, sailing on a broad-reach, et cetera.

Remember, easy-does-it with jibing. The wind will pick you up lickity-split as you turn. Be prepared!

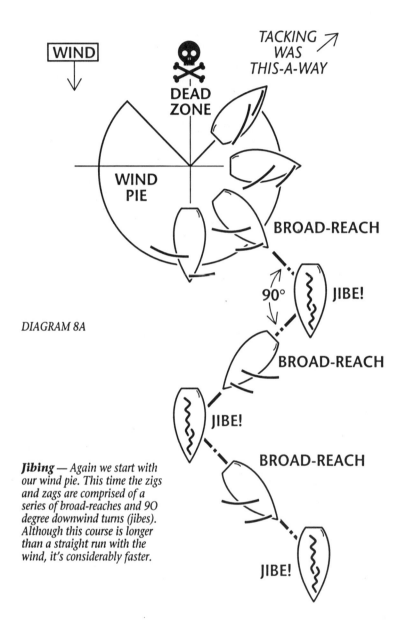

WIND

TACKING
WAS
THIS-A-WAY

DEAD
ZONE

WIND
PIE

BROAD-REACH

90° JIBE!

DIAGRAM 8A

BROAD-REACH

JIBE!

BROAD-REACH

Jibing — *Again we start with our wind pie. This time the zigs and zags are comprised of a series of broad-reaches and 90 degree downwind turns (jibes). Although this course is longer than a straight run with the wind, it's considerably faster.*

JIBE!

__Jibing__ — Cliff and Connie begin their jibe from a broad-reach.

Cliff slowly pulls the tiller towards himself.

As the boat swings around...

... all eyes are on the boom.

more pix ⇾

This is the critical part of the turn (jibe). The wind is blowing straight over the stern and will catch the main sail any moment.

Cliff and Connie release their sheets and...thar she goes! As the boom swoops over their heads, they switch sides.

Connie and Cliff adjust and trim their sails to suit the new course.

Note that Cliff has hold of the tiller throughout this sequence, maintaining a steady turn.

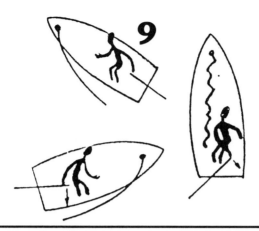

UPWIND SAILING

Remember that frightening diagram in the class-room chapter? The one with all the zigzags coming out of the wind pie? Well, that's the symbology of sailing into the wind--the art of sailing close-hauled and tacking.

(Oh, by the way. Although one may say reach-ING, and runn-ING, and broad-reach-ING, one cannot say close-haul-ING. There is no present participle for this particular point of sail. Why? THE CODE.)

Sailing Close-Hauled

The reality of that diagram is a lot easier to understand in a boat. Put yourself into a reach. Now slowly steer the boat into the wind while sheeting in. Keep turning until you see the luff of the jib begin to flap. As soon as you do, turn the boat ever so slightly back again--just so that sail tension is regained. You are now sailing close-hauled, 45 degrees off the wind source. As close as a sailor can get to the dead zone and still move. As close as a sailor can ever get to sailing upwind.

Since you're always headed upwind at best at a 45 degree angle, in order to reach an upwind bearing you must execute a series of 90 degree angle turns to get there. Hence all the zigzagging. The zigs and zags are sailed close-hauled. Turning into a zig or zag is called a tack.

Tacking

Tacking is pushing the tiller away from you and turning the boat until the sail and boom swing around and catch the wind from the other side. Sounds simple, and it is in theory, but there's a trick or two to it.

First off, try a tack from a reach. You'll have more speed to turn you through the dead zone. So to tack...

1) Look and make sure you're not turning into a party boat..

2) Build up your speed...

3) Push the tiller away from you...

4) Release both sails (uncleat jib and main sails)...

5) Switch sides and DUCK as the boom swings around...

6) Set your sails (cleat jib and haul in main)...

7) Find your close-hauled course and get a bearing on the shore.

Close-hauled — *The boat is sailing as close to an upwind direction as possible. Straight upwind is just off to Cliff's left (port). Sails are hauled in close (get it?) in order to maximize trim.*

Tacking — *Making it look easy. Cliff begins his turn from a close-haul by pushing the tiller away.*

Chapter Nine

The boat is pointed directly into the dead zone.

Cliff maintains his turn on the tiller.

As the boom swings around they switch sides...

...and readjust their sails.

Backwinding — *The boat is caught in irons- pointed straight into the wind and stopped dead. Connie pushes the main sail out in order to catch some wind.*

While Connie holds the sail out, Cliff pulls the tiller over. The boat begins to back into a turn.

The boat has backed into a point of sail. Connie quickly seats herself as the main sail catches and the boom swings around.

They're back in business.

Got all that? Don't sweat it. This takes practice. Tacking is like learning how to turn on skis or on a snowboard. It's somewhat elusive and difficult until.. it isn't. For now you're gonna do a little stumbling and grumbling. You'll do donuts. You'll tangle the sheets. You'll stop dead in the dead zone. But all that's OK. Just don't go boom on da boom. That could ruin your whole day.

Ideally you want to work into an upwind course that goes from close-hauled to a tack, close-hauled to a tack, close-hauled, et cetera. Just like the zigzag diagrams. You'll have a tendency to turn too far over in the beginning and tack into a reach. It'll take awhile to get your rhythm down, but with practice, practice, practice, you too will become a Tackmeister Supreme.

Caught in Irons

Let's say in your tack you become stuck in the dead zone. That is, the boat is pointed straight into the wind, the sails are luffing like crazy, and you're not moving anywhere. Using another (rather imaginative) phrase, you are 'caught in irons.' This is a common enough occurrence and easy to remedy.

Just push the rudder all the way over and push out the boom so that the wind can hit the sail. The boat will back into a point of sail from which you can regain momentum and try the tack again.

Upwind Sailing

DOCKING

Well look at you... You can sail north and south, east and west, no matter which way the wind blows! So what if you're a little ragged. Where's the lanes out there, anyway? Where's the doggone road for that matter. Let's go back and do a little braggadocio!

Uh, oh. Dock Time.

This could be your worst moment. Prepare yourself. Nobody saw you sail so splendidly out there, but everybody's gonna see you tear into the dock. Or miss it. Suffice it to say that docking your sailboat is one of those character building endeavors in life. Like the first time you tried to parallel park.

Docking is another timing thing. What you do is simple. Exactly when you do it is another matter. However, if you read the wind properly, chances are you'll do fine. Really.

Docking

Docking *— Sailing in slowly with sails out.*

Turning upwind into the docking area.

Sheets are released.

Sliding ever so gently next to the dock.

This pix says it all about docking. As they dock the bow is pointed upwind and both sheets are released. The boat is moving just fast enough to park itself next to the dock. (NEXT TO is the key phrase here— as opposed to AWAY FROM or INTO.)

Figure out which way the wind is blowing to your dock. You want to end your glide into the dock going upwind. Barely moving. Never, ever try to land with the wind. You'll crash and burn for sure.

Eyeball the place you want to end up on the dock and aim for a spot two boat lengths downwind of it. As you approach, let the sails completely out. When you hit your 'spot', turn upwind and gently slide into the dock.

Obviously, it's better to have too little momentum than too much. Someone can always throw you a rope or you can try again if you fall short. But crashing is, well, crashing.

Before you set out ask a local sailor the best way to deal with the dock. Each one has its own nuances.

My Favorite Docking Story

Docking sailboats can be a hassle but as long as you avoid doing this one thing, chances are it won't be a catastrophe. DO NOT ATTEMPT TO DOCK UNDER FULL SAIL. It's like easing into a parking place at 40 miles an hour.

I had had my first boat for about, oh, two weeks and had fallen in love with it and with sailing. Up to this point in time, I had never dealt with a dock, always having launched and landed from a beach. But on this day I was leaving from, and returning to, a dock. The leaving was a piece of cake. It was the arriving that became epic.

Not knowing that there might be a trick to this docking business, I was returning from a short jaunt in the bay on a reach with a moderate wind. I have no idea what I was thinking at the time. It didn't register that there might be a problem until I was practically on top of the dock.

Thoughts like 'Gee, I'm going kinda fast. How am I gonna stop this thing?' flashed through my mind before it shut down entirely and I was forced to react to the impending danger with jungle reflexes alone.

With the dock looming in front of me, I cranked my craft alongside the dock at about 75 miles per hour, looped my feet under the hiking strap in the cockpit, lunged towards one of the pilings speeding by, and hugged it with all my might.

It was like Buster Keaton. Or more accurately, like some sort of cartoon because I'm sure I was stretching out like an elastic band.

I'm holding on to this piling with my arms and barely hanging on to this bucking boat with my toenails. I'm bridged over about five feet of water, losing my grip, and hoping nobody is witnessing all this... when the cavalry came.

It was Rich. Owner of said dock. He grabbed the boat, uncleated the sail and reeled me in. Afterward, in that calm, easy going way of his, he explained how I should have approached the dock--into the wind, or upwind, with sails loose. And perhaps a tad slower. We both agreed that it was time for a little instruction.

I tell you this story because it illustrates the need to know something about the ways of the wind before you wing it. When you're thrashing about in the open water you can learn by trial and error without serious consequence. In fact, that's a great way to learn about 95% of all this stuff. But when you're around other boats and/or the dock it's time for control. And in order to have control a sailor needs to master basic skills. Learn them!

Docking

11

CAN YOU GUESS WHAT THE BATTLESHIP RULE IS?

RULES OF THE ROAD

It's a lot simpler than you might think...

1) *The Starboard Rule* (see diagram 11a)

If two boats approach each other from opposite directions, the boat on a starboard tack has right-of-way over the boat on a port tack.

A Starboard tack is when the wind blows into (over) your starboard (right) side.

A Port tack is when the wind blows into (over) your port (left) side

There is no particular reason for the starboard tack to supersede the port tack. It's just that way.

DIAGRAM 11A

Starboard Rule —
Starboard tack has right-of-way.

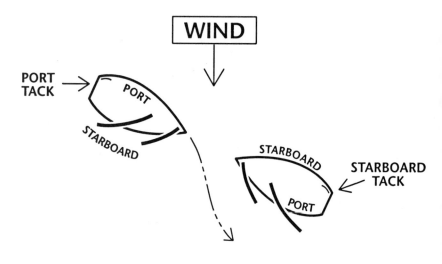

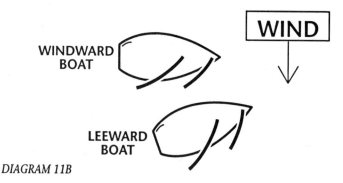

DIAGRAM 11B

Windward/Leeward Rule —
Leeward boat has right-of-way.

2) *The Windward/Leeward Rule*

(see diagram 11b)

If two boats are traveling in the same direction, the leeward boat has right-of-way over the windward boat.

The windward boat is the boat the wind hits first.

The leeward boat is the boat the wind hits after the windward boat.

There is a reason for this rule. The windward boat has more wind to work with than the leeward boat. Since the windward boat is receiving wind first it may be blocking the wind from the leeward boat. Thus, the windward boat has more control.

Windward, by the way, is pronounced like it looks. Leeward, however, is pronounced loo-erd. But the word 'lee' by itself is pronounced lee, just like it looks.

This is yet another example of THE CODE. Why loo for lee with -erd, and lee for lee without? No reason. But watch the eyebrows pop if you say lee-ward instead of loo-erd. No cocktails in the Captain's Room for you tonight!

3) *The Overtaking Rule*

If two boats are headed in the same direction, the slower boat has right-of-way. The overtaking boat gives way to the overtaken boat. The faster boat is assumed to have more control.

4) *The Power Boat Rule*

All power boats 65' or less must give way to sailboats. Power boats have more control than a sailboat up to a point. When they get closer to aircraft carrier size, they don't. That means you get out of THEIR way!

5) *The Courtesy Rule*

Even if you have right-of-way, you must avoid the other boat. In other words, don't run into anybody.

At least remember this one. In fact, for now, just stay away from everybody and everything.

The Bridge That Wouldn't Budge

Knowing the rules of the road is very important, indeed. However it's just as important to know the road.

A very good friend of mine was sailing the inland waterway in Florida for the first time when his fellow sailor pointed out a draw bridge ahead. The bridge seemed a little low for the mast and it was probable that it would have to be drawn up in order for them to pass.

Ahead of them a ways was a much larger vessel. It most certainly would need the bridge to lift. My friend and his mate looked on to see how the first boat dealt with the situation.

As it closed in, they heard three sharp blasts from a horn and, like 'open sesame', the bridge lifted and let the boat pass. In a minute or so, the bridge came back down.

No problemo. Toot the horn thrice and the gates open. Got it.

In time their sailboat was upon the bridge. They tooted the horn and prepared to whisk on through.

The bridge didn't budge.

They blasted three more times. Not a crack.

Meanwhile, of course, their boat was getting mighty close to the bridge. And sure enough, the mast was a good five feet taller than the underpass. Now this sailboat was pretty big and pretty expensive. Masts on these puppies cost a mint. Breaking one tends to dampen the spirits of yachtsmen in no small way. And from the looks of things, that's exactly what was in store unless some speedy seamanship commenced pronto.

With his buddy blasting nonstop on the airhorn, yelling and waving at the bridgemaster's shack (that's what it was, wasn't it?), my pal cranked the boat around and desperately tried to hightail it back before the mast hit. Needless to say, since sailboats can't respond to directional changes like a power boat, the situation was going to be tight.

With the mast inches from destruction and both sailors in a frenzied kind of praying-cursing-accusing mode, the drawbridge decided to raise up. Mast and boat glided through. Unscathed.

As they floated through to the other side, they noticed a sign on the bridge:

DRAWBRIDGE OPENS AUTOMATICALLY EVERY 15 MINUTES. LISTEN FOR 3 HORN BLASTS.

When there's no traffic, you don't have to worry about rules. In the beginning, it's best to stay away from everything and everybody.

SOME PHYSICS

What makes a sailboat go is a little more than the wind pushing against the sails. It can actually get quite technical if you're racing a 50 million dollar vessel, but for our purposes, there are just a couple feats of physics I'll get into here.

The Sail is a Foil (See diagram 12a)

The only time the sail acts as a mere wind catcher, when the wind is simply pushing boat and sail along, is when the boat is running with the wind.

In any other direction (except the dead zone, of course), the sails are functioning as foils. Pretty much like an airplane wing.

Pictured are a sail (from above), and an airplane wing (from the side). Around each is a flow of air particles. The flow around the sail is caused by the wind. The flow around the wing is caused by the

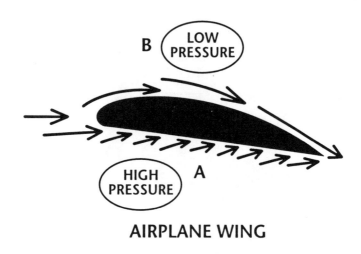

AIRPLANE WING

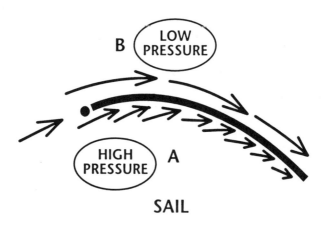

SAIL

DIAGRAM 12A

The Bernoulis Principle — *Moving air splits itself above and below the foil shapes. The air below the foils becomes condensed and creates high pressure systems that push into the low pressure areas above. This gives the wing its lift and your sail its shove.*

movement of the airplane through the air. In both cases the air particles are split by either the leading edge of the sail (the mast), or the wing. As it's illustrated here, some of the particles go over the sail and wing (the 'B' particles), and some go under (the 'A' particles).

In both diagrams the 'B' particles have a longer distance to travel than the 'A' particles. This is due to the curving back of the foil shape around which they are traveling. These particles are less condensed than the 'A' particles, which are getting sorta jammed up along the opposite side. All this jamming creates a higher pressure on this side than the other. It's this higher pressure on one side, in combination with the lower pressure on the other, that provides the push on the sail and the lift on a wing.

This is called the Bernoulis Principle.

Sail Angles

It follows that the angle of the sail can play an important role in all this particle pressure. As a sailor pulls in his sails on a reach, for example, he or she increases the pressure on the windward side of the sails and decreases the pressure on the leeward side. The result is increased boat speed and perhaps a pronounced tilt to lee.

Of course, there is a point where these physics are lost if the sailor pulls the sails in too much. There is an optimum setting for any point of sail.

Conversely, letting out the sails decreases the pressure on the windward side of the sails and results in a loss of speed.

Now all of this means nothing if you haven't got a daggerboard or centerboard.

The Daggerboard/Centerboard

The daggerboard/centerboard plays an integral role in moving your sailboat in all directions except downwind. Like I said, when the boat is moving downwind, the physics of motion is merely that of the wind pushing boat and sail. No foil. No split particles. No high or low pressures. You're just being shoved. That's why it's so slow.

The centerboard prevents the wind from shoving the boat leeward (with the wind) when the boat is pointed anywhere else. On a reach the wind hits the sail and boat broadside, but can't shove the boat that way because the centerboard pins the boat down. It makes the boat go in the direction the rudder tells it--the path of least resistance. Take the daggerboard out on a reach and the boat will blow with the wind. Without a daggerboard/centerboard a boat can only be sailed with the wind.

Now do you see why I put this theory stuff here?

Unless you design rockets for a living, it takes a wrenching of the brain muscle to plow through some of the finer points. I figured if I tried to explain the whys behind the hows all at once, folks would either doze off or start to weep uncontrollably. Especially when you're expecting light reading about fun boat rides.

Not to worry. Knowing theory won't sail your boat. Although some of it is good to know, and it can be interesting in a left-side-of-the-brain kinda way, it's better to get out there and plow around as soon as you can. It's the seeing and feeling and doing that'll pull you through. And those things won't happen sitting in a classroom. (Thank God!)

13

RIGGING

If you're renting your sailboat chances are you won't have to set it up, or rig it. However, sooner or later you're going to have to learn. It's a step-by-step kind of thing. Not really very difficult at all.

At this point assume the boat is in the water, the mast is raised and secured by its wire shrouds.

1) Plug in the plug at the stern.

2) Slip in the centerboard next. It helps to stabilize the boat as you stumble on, off, and around it during the rigging ritual.

3) Attach the rudder to the pins on the outside of the stern. Make sure it passes underneath the ropes back there that attach to the boom (the traveler). Secure it with the rope or cord attachment.

4) Untie or unclasp the main halyard (rope that pulls up the main sail) from the end of the boom. Unfurl the main sail and attach the halyard to the tip-top of the main sail. Use a bowline knot if there isn't a shackle.

5) Make sure the main sheet is uncleated. Look up and check your main halyard for tangles or fouling. As you pull up the main sail, feed the luff into the slot on the mast. Pull the sail all the up and tie down your end of the halyard to the cleat at the base of the mast. Use a cleat knot. Coil the remaining rope and stuff it 'tween the mast and halyard

6) Look at your main sail and check for sagging along the mast and boom. It should be pulled tight. If you need to adjust the tension along the boom, use the outhaul line located on the boom. If the tension along the mast is lacking, use the downhaul line located at the base of the mast.

7) Unwrap the jib and hook the bottom to the hook on the bow. Starting at the bottom, fasten the little jib do-hickies to the fore stay.

8) Now take the jib sheets around the shrouds. One on each side of the boat, of course. Poke the ends of each through the cleats and tie them in figure eight knots. Don't cleat them down.

9) Untie the jib halyard at the mast and attach the shackle to the tip-top of the jib sail. Pull the jib all the way up until the fore stay is slightly slack. Cleat the jib halyard with a cleat knot on its cleat at the base of the mast. (Say THAT fast a few times.)

There you go! You should be ready to make sailing history. Make sure all your lines are coiled and stowed out of the way, that you have knots at the end of all your sheets, and that everything that you fiddled with is tied down tight. In other words, make sure you're shipshape, mate.

Rigging Illustrated

Plugging in the plug.

Sliding in the daggerboard.

Attaching the rudder.

Unclasping the main halyard (rope that pulls up the main sail) from the boom.

more pix➤

Unfurling the main sail.

Attaching the main halyard to the top of the mast.

Checking for tangles.

Sliding the main sail into the slot on the mast.

Hauling up the main sail. Make sure the main sheet is uncleated.

Cleating down the main halyard. See page 89 for knot.

Neatly coiled and stowed.

Checking for sagging along the boom and mast.

more pix➤

Adjusting the outhaul for sagging along the boom.

Adjusting the downhaul for sagging along the mast.

Hooking the bottom of the jib to the bow.

Fastening the jib to the fore stay (the wire stretching from bow to mast top).

Jib sheets go around the shrouds (the wires holding up the mast)...

...and through their respective cleats. Tie the ends in figure eight knots. See page 90 for knot. Do not cleat.

Attaching the jib halyard to the top of the jib.

Hauling up the jib.

more pix→

*OK. Step back and take a look. Sails should be pulled all the way up and out.
No sags.*

Cleat Knot — *For cleating down the halyards.*

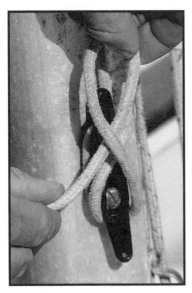

Figure Eight Knot — *For tying off the jib sheets.*

Bowline Knot — *For attaching a line to anything. This knot does not slip.*

more pix ⤳

Bowline Knot — *(continued)*

Special Note

Your boat may very well be different than the one we rigged here. You might not have a jib. Or shrouds. Some stuff isn't going to attach or tie down or look exactly like it's shown and described here.

But then again, a lot of it should be similar. Or similar enough for you to piece a small monohull of most any type together without too much fret and sweat. Obviously, advice and real-live instruction is always a good idea if it continues to be a jumble.

And do remember this. Everything about rigging makes perfect sense. Always. No matter what boat. It's one of the beauties of sailing. Perhaps the inane jargon is somewhat confusing and convoluted, but the way your little boat is meant to be put together is precise. And once understood, simple.

14

SAFETY

BE AWARE. BE PREPARED. HEY, DON'T BE STUPID!

1) *Know how to swim.*

Since most of your sailing will occur in large bodies of water, this is an important point.

2) *Watch where you're going.*

And everywhere else. All the time.

3) *Know the waters.*

Be aware of what you're sailing through. Know the currents, the bottom, the traffic, the winds, the weather...And be prepared.

Just a bad day all around. Rocks, waves, and much, too much wind. And leave the relatives at home!

Chapter Fourteen

4) *Respect the weather.*

It's bigger 'n you.

5) *Know your limitations.*

The sea (or bay, or lake, or river) is a fickle lady. (Can I say that?) The price for overconfidence can be high. Make sure you can handle the conditions at hand. Make sure you can handle a certain type of boat before you set out in it.

6) *Make sure vessel and gear are sound.*

Yes, boats still sink and lines still snap. 'Ship-shape' is a boating term that, unlike some of its cousins, makes all the sense in the world.

7) *Watch your head!*

Or to be more precise, watch out for the boom as it swings around.

8) *Life preservers*

One per sailor.

Sailing really is a common sensical endeavor. Whether learning it or practicing it. Play it safe. Use your head.

Safety

THE CAPTAIN BLIGH
SYNDROME (CBS)*

I saw this Goldie Hawn movie once. It was a comedy about some rich guy and his wife (Goldie) sailing around the world in their huge yacht. There was this one scene where he was at the helm and having a fierce argument with Goldie. He wanted to go here but she wanted to go there. The fight escalated to a point where he threatened to toss her overboard. She laughed and said he wouldn't dare. His response was classic CBS:

"I can do whatever I want. Once at sea, a captain is God!"

---

* *Captain Bligh was the cap'n who gave Clark Gable, Marlon Brando, and later Mel Gibson such a rough time during a couple of boat rides on the Bounty.*

It was meant to be funny, of course, but like a lotta humor it touched very close to something that isn't very funny at all when one is on the receiving end.

Anyone who has ever sailed knows exactly what I'm speaking about. It has something to do with the tiller. Whomever touches it becomes 'CAPTAIN.' If he\she is allowed to keep it for any length of time, a personality change ensues that in stages becomes blunt, gruff, and finally maddog. In no time at all an otherwise docile human being will become an Ahab. An Admiral Nelson. A Captain Blood. And woe to the hapless crew who must serve him\her!

It reminds me of that old Goofy cartoon. The one in which he's a mild-mannered family man until he gets behind the wheel of his car. There he turns into this raving lunatic--screeching and speeding his auto out of the neighborhood, blowing other cars off the road; screaming and shaking his fist until he pulls into his parking place at the office. He then re-transforms himself into the gentle soul he normally is.

What is it about boats and mad caps, anyway? Why do everyday 'nice' people turn into such blazing buttheads on the high seas? Maybe it's the confined space. Maybe it's too many Errol Flynn movies. Maybe they just think they can get away with it. Like the open waters are some kind of frontier where civilized behavior is optional. Whatever the reason, I've seen and heard about lots of sailing sorties that have turned ugly because the CAPTAIN got fat in the head.

Like THE CODE, wet sneakers and barnacles, CBS ain't goin' away anytime soon. All you can do is try to avoid it. Stay away from:

Chapter Fifteen

1) Anyone dressed in a blue blazer, matching white turtle neck and trousers, and yachting cap. This, obviously enough, indicates a troubled mind, but if his\her boat is only 14' long, you know you're dealing with chronic CBS.

2) Anyone drinking gin out of the bottle before 10 am.

3) Anyone rattling ball bearings and mumbling incoherently.

4) Anyone wearing a saber and\or a Napoleon bonnet

The list goes on yet it's the normal-looking ones, the people you know and trust, who'll get you every time. And here's the grabber. THERE IS NOTHING YOU CAN DO ABOUT IT! As long as you accept boat rides on other people's boats, you are at risk. As long as you remain a novice to the sailing game, you will be at the mercy of those demented individuals who grow horns at the tiller. There is no running away...

Unless you take this sailing business to heart and learn how to skipper your own boat. Then you can set the rules. Then you can be the sensitive, caring, patient cap'n that everyone will admire and point to and say 'Look! There's the skipper who isn't a jerk. I sure wish my daddy (or mommie or husband or wife or whomever) was more like him\her!

Or you can be-your-own-Bligh. And seek vengeance like the rest of us.

Happy sailing!

Captain Bligh Syndrome

16

CATS!

Some of you are getting itchy. You've seen the beer commercials with the guy hanging waaaaay out over the water sailing a boat that looks a lot different than your sloop. He's got the thing nearly upended and he's tracking at warp speed.

You wanna try one of those.

Catamarans or 'cats' are probably what you have in mind. As previously mentioned, catamarans have two hulls. On any given day, they're the fastest sailboats in the water. As a matter of fact, cats can speed up to 25 knots or more. That's twice as fast as the sleekest monohull. The little boat you learned in can only go about 3 knots.

The physics behind all this mostly involves sail area and boat weight. Cats are relatively light and have huge sails. Monohulls are heavier. Cats get moving so fast that they create their own wind. But more on that later.

Let's get out on one first...Right after you read this:

The Cat Qualification for Beginners (CQB)

You have enough knowledge and skill at this point to manage or begin to learn to manage a catamaran in light to moderate wind. That's like 8 knots or less. You should be able to take off, come back in, locate and negotiate the points of sail (the wind pie applies just the same), including tacking, even fly a hull, without much problem.

BUT...

Stay away from heavier winds. Cats can really fly in and out of the water. They are built to charge. It takes a might more know-how than you now have to safely address anything more than a stiff breeze.

Your initial cat rides will probably be on a 16 or 18 foot boat. These are the most common sizes.

What's Different About Cats?

(BESIDES the fact that they have two skinny hulls that you'll want to call pontoons. But don't EVER call them that in front of an experienced cat sailor).

1) Getting Wet
Prepare for a dousing spray and butt soaks.

2) Awright! No Docks!
That's right sailor peoples. You can take off from and land on the beach. They're made to do just that. Usually that's how you'll find them at sailing areas.

Big sails and light hulls equal speed!

Cats!

Cats are beached, not docked.

3) *What! No Seats?*

No seats or sides on these puppies. Cats have a trampoline-like platform (called a trampoline) made of stretched canvas upon which you'll scramble and sit. There are straps to scoot your feet under and not much of anything else.

4) *No Centerboard*

The function of a centerboard is incorporated into the hull design of entry-level cats.

5) *Two Rudders*

One behind each hull. There's a bar contraption or rope dealies that pops 'em up and down. When you smash into the beach they'll pop up without damage.

6) *A Long, Cumbersome Pole*

The tiller is a long pole. You fit it under your armpit. It's kinda awkward during a tack because of all the length. You have to swing it out and around each time you change sides. It's long so you can always have a hold of it as you move about or out on a hike.

7) *Endless Sheets*

The sails are managed the same as your monohull's. It's just that the sheets have no ends. They're big loops of rope that run through the cleats. And that's cool--no loose ends.

8) *Trimming*

It's pretty much the same as before. Pull 'em in and let 'em out. You'll find that in a cat the sails will want to be pulled in closer when you're close-hauled and on broad-reaches than in the monohull.

Sheets are one continuous loop.

Cats have long tillers in order to reach hiking, scrambling sailors.

9) *WHOA! It's FAST!*

Once you've pushed off, set the sails, and caught a little wind, you'll notice THE DIFFERENCE right away. Make no mistake about it. Cats are built for SPEED.

10) *WHOA! This is REALLY FUN!*

And you're so CLOSE to the water. Or so it seems because you can see it RUSHING underneath through the webbing. And since there aren't any sides, it's like your on this speeding carpet ride slicing through the water. Yes, INDEED! Without a doubt, cats are the sexy, sizzling, HOTdogging side of small boat sailing.

11) *WHOA! FLYING A HULL!*

Now get set in a reach. If there's enough wind, your windward hull (the one you're sitting over) will want to rise out of the water. And UP you'll go! THIS is a supreme blast. Tearing along on one hull, balancing just so that you maintain maximum trim and thrust (hull is 3 to 6 inches out of the water) is one of the sweeter sweetspots in cat sailing.

It's also a workout. The mainsail is big, catches alotta wind and be tuff to sheet in. The boat is going so fast that maintaining a bearing on a maxed-out reach is like wrestling a baby rhino. And you thought sailing was a finesse sport. Best pump some iron, sailor!

Remember: WHEN IN DOUBT--LET 'EM OUT! If it feels like you're gonna be catapulted, just let out the main sail like you did in the monohull.

Flying a hull!

Capsize Recovery *— The sheets are released. Cliff tosses the righting rope over the upended hull...*

...and catches it on the other side.

Cliff and Tom commence to pulling...

...and pulling...

more pix ➤

Cats!

...and pulling...

Finally the sails pop free of the drink.

The cat rights itself...

...and plops over their heads.

12) *Downwind Sailing*

Running directly with the wind in a cat is slow. You do it just like you did in the monohull.

It's faster to sail towards your bearing in a series of broad-reaches, again, like you did in the sloop. Even though your zigzagging course is much longer than a straight run, your cat will cover the distance in much shorter time.

13) *Don't Capsize*

This is a major hassle. You can't right yourself by yourself. It takes 325 lbs. and a tussle to get a cat back upright. If you stay out of the strong winds and monitor your main sail properly you should be fine.

But here's what you do if you end-o...

A) Uncleat the sheets.

B) Locate the righting rope underneath the trampoline.

C) Toss the rope over the upended hull.

D) Both sailors grab hold, stand on the bottom hull and puuulll! The cat will plop over and settle over your head.

14) *Tacking (This one deserves its own chapter...)*

Cats!

17

TACKING IN A CAT

This you'll have to relearn. Tacking is slow-going in a cat. They're not built to come about quickly or efficiently. In fact, the hassle in coming about in a cat is not coming about at all, or getting stuck in the dead zone (caught in irons).

Here are the ABC's of cat tacking:

A) Achieve a close-hauled course. You want the cat to have as little distance to swing around as possible. When a cat isn't going in a straight line it just wants to squat and die.

B) Push the tiller away slowly and don't let go. Cats do not respond well to abrupt directional change. It'll stop. Of course, if the tiller isn't held to a steady course the boat will cease its pivot.

Do not release the sheets, yet.

C) As the boat swings around the jib will begin to pick up the wind from the other side and help push you all the way 'round. This is called backwinding. It's more or less the jib that does the work in a cat tack.

D) Release the main sheet and switch sides. Remember to hold on to the tiller and to keep it turned the way you want to go. It's easy to lose control now, what with the long-poled tiller and all. It has to swing out and around underneath the boom. It's awkward but since the tack is so slow you should have plenty of fumbling time.

E) The main sail will 'pop' as it fills with wind. Grab hold of the main sheet.

F) Release the jib (at last) and set it on the other side.

G) And away you'll go. Or perhaps I should say ZOOM! Cats are definitely off-track on a tack, but point them in the right direction and in no time you're flying.

Take note that the main sail is dormant throughout the tack. If it becomes involved too soon it'll counteract the push upon the jib and spin you back.

You will get stuck in the dead zone more frequently in a cat than in a monohull. If you get caught in irons, push the rudder over and push the boom out as you did in the sloop. You'll back out of the stall into a point of sail from which you can try another tack.

As you can see, it's this tacking business that requires the most schooling when you graduate from monohull to catamaran. (Up to this point, anyway.) As you progress and deal with greater wind there will be much more to absorb. Believe it.

Chapter Seventeen

Cat Tack — *Cliff and Connie prepare to tack from a close-haul.*

Cliff slowly pushes the tiller away.

Slowly and steadily the boat comes around.

The cat is pointed directly into the dead zone. Note the jib is picking up the wind.

more pix ➤

It's the jib that helps complete the turn at this point. The main sheet is released and our sailors switch sides.

Mr. Jib is still working away while the main sail remains dormant. Cliff cranks the tiller out and around, still maintaining the turn.

Cliff and Connie settle in as the boat chugs around.

'POP!' goes the main sail as it finally catches. Connie releases the jib sheet and sets it on the other side. Cliff has hold of the main sheet and prepares to take off.

18

CAT PHYSICS

* *Again, I'm just scratching the surface with this theory stuff — just enough to give y'all an idea of what's what.*

Big sails on a light hull equals speed.

And all this speed makes for what is called 'created wind'--like the wind your car makes when it speeds forward. Stick your hand out and you feel created wind. Your monohull's forward progress wasn't great enough to produce much of any.

Here comes the theory part (see diagram 18a). The mean 'tween the real wind (as in where the natural wind is blowing from), and the created wind (the wind blowing over the bow as you move), is called 'apparent wind'. Apparent wind is the distillation of real and created wind that actually reacts with your cat's sails and makes you move.

OK. See the angle of the apparent wind as it hits your cat? It's a lot sharper than the angle the real wind made against your monohull sail. Apparent wind is more straight on.

In order for a sail to work in apparent wind, it must be less foiled, or flatter than a monohull's sail (see diagram 18b). The straight-on nature of apparent wind will buckle the foil of a bulging monohull sail and render it a flapping, useless mess. In order to flatten cat sails, battens are strung all the way through the width of the sail. This also makes them stiff enough to hold their flat shape as well. It's all this stiffness that makes a cat's sail 'pop' when you tack.

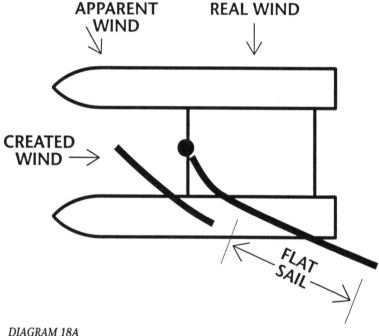

DIAGRAM 18A

Catamarans are so fast that they create their own wind—called apparent wind. Cat sails are flatter, less foiled than monohull sails in order to deal with the angle of apparent wind.

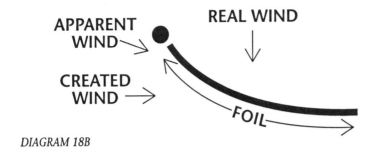

DIAGRAM 18B

The foil shape of a monohull's sail wouldn't work on a cat. The apparent wind would buckle the foil and render it useless.

The catamaran hull functions as a centerboard on entry-level models. The outside is flat and the inside curvaceous. (Curvaceous?)

No Centerboard

The inside of each hull is flat on entry-level cats. The design functions like the centerboard in a monohull.

Maximum Trim

...is achieved when one hull is in the water and the other is 3 to 6 inches out. One hull in the water is less resistant than two. But going too high prevents the wind from reacting with the sail at an optimum angle.

Maximum trim also requires that the waterline around your hull(s) is even. Avoid having your hull(s) dip down (pitch-pulling) or ride up. You balance things out by placing your weight properly and monitoring your main sail.

Tacking

Tacking is slow going because one of the hulls is resisting the movement. Instead of one hull pivoting and turning both, a cat has one pivoting and the other trying to pivot around it.

Special Note or Repeating-Myself-'Cause-It's-Important

Cat sailing isn't all that easy. Or it's easy until it isn't and then all hell breaks loose. This chapter is meant to whet your appetite. That's all. Take lessons and learn from a pro. Yeah, you can give it a go in light winds, but catamarans can get real spooky and scary when it starts to blow. Know your limitations!

Chapter Eighteen

Cat Sails — *Big, flat, and battened.*

Cat in Trim — *One hull is raised (flying) slightly above the water. With one hull in the water instead of two, there is less resistance. Thus more thrust.*

Zoning in a Cat

I'll never forget the first time I took a cat out in the ocean.

The wind was light on the bay as we sailed toward the inlet. So light we barely made it. Then we finally saw the sea...

Once in the inlet, the swells marched underneath us like a bunch of rolling hills. Gently bucking us up and down. WAY up and WAY down. The open ocean was starting to look and feel real BIG.

Then the wind hit. Outside the protected bay the prevailing wind had nothing to slow it down. And away we went--like zero to sixty in five seconds. The sails popped and the boat actually started to hum. The hull we were sitting over lifted and we assumed that hanging-over-the-side position you see in all the magazines-- without even thinking about it.

I was mesmerized by the power. The hulls cut through the chop like a speedboat. Looking back, each rudder was spewing a rooster-tail. Holding on to sheet and tiller was a job for the hulkster.

We got going so fast that the boat bolted practically upright. I slid down the trampoline, underneath the hiking strap, up to my armpits. For a second or two we were sailing on END with me in this semi-crucifix and my buddy sitting on the SIDE of the uplifted hull. It certainly felt like curtains. (How do you right one of these things?) In the nick of time I managed to let out the main and we plopped back down.

Whew! What a ride! After a while I got a feel for the lift of the hull together with the proper sail tension. Balancing things just so in order to maintain this hair-raising thrust through the water. Man, I was in the ZONE! I never dreamed that sailing could be such rip-roaring, limb-wrenching, rolly-coaster ride!

Different Strokes

Now obviously catamaran sailing isn't for everybody. And I'm sure that after reading the previous ditty many of you will begin to ascertain your own feelings about high performance sailing. Some of you are gonna water at the mouth and give it a try. But many of you will want to pass.

And that's OK.

Because this is a fact: If there's a sport with variety, it's sailing. It can be fast or slow or thrilling or laid-back or wet or dry or ANYTHING YOU WANT IT TO BE. And somewhere there's a boat just for you to do just those very things.

Guaranteed.

THAT'S ALL..

...I'm gonna teach you. One thing about sailing--there's always something else to learn. All this is just scratching the surface. There's a zillion different boats and a zillion different ways in which to sail them. And every time you go out there's a different set of conditions to challenge you.

So keep at it, avoid CBS, and have some fun out there. After all, that's what sailing is all about!

Cat Physics

GLOSSARY

A sailing glossary could easily fill a book. What you have here is pretty much what you oughta know.

Aft — A part of the boat at or near the stern.

Apparent Wind — Associated with catamaran sailing. The mean between real and created wind.

Backwinding — When caught in irons, pushing boom and main sail out in order to catch wind and back into a point of sail.

Battens — The thin strips of wood/fiberglass that fit into and stiffen sails.

Bearing — The point a sailor chooses to sail towards.

Bernoulis Principle — A major part of sailing theory/physics. Explains how a sail works.

Boom — The wood/metal beam attached to the mast and mainsail.

Bow — The front of the boat.

Bowline — A common knot in sailing. Noteworthy in that it never slips .

Broad-Reach — A direction or point of sail 135 degrees from the wind source.

Catamaran — A boat with two hulls.

Cat — Catamaran

Capsize — To turn a boat over.

Caught in Irons — A situation in which the bow is pointed upwind and the boat cannot move forward or turn.

CBS — Captain Bligh Syndrome. A common personality disorder associated with ship command.

Centerboard — A pivoting stabilizing member located underneath the hull.

Cleat — A fitting used to secure lines.

Cleat Knot — The knot used to tie lines to cleats.

Close-Haul — A direction or point of sail 45 degrees from the wind source.

Created Wind — The wind created from forward movement. Associated with catamaran sailing.

Daggerboard — A stabilizing member located underneath the hull that slides in and out.

Dead Zone — That direction 45 degrees to either side of the wind source in which sailing is impossible. AKA luffing or no sail zone.

Downhaul — The line that adjusts vertical tension in the main sail.

Downwind — A direction with the wind, away from the wind source.

Flying a Hull — Associated with catamaran sailing. When one hull lifts up and out of the water, usually on a reach.

Fore — A part of a boat at or near the bow.

Fore Stay — The wire mast support attached to the bow.

Halyard — The line that hauls up the sail.

Hull — The body of the boat.

Jib Sail — The smaller sail attached to the bow.

Jibing — Turning with the wind on a downwind course by pulling the tiller in or away from the sail(s).

Knot — A nautical unit of speed equaling 1.15 MPH.

Laser — Make of a small, single sail boat known for its maneuverability.

Leeward — Pronounced loo-erd. Situated or moving away from the wind source.

Luff — Leading edge of a sail. Also a verb— the flapping of untrimmed sails.

Main Sail — The bigger sail attached to the boom.

Mast — The big pole holding up the sails.

Monohull — A boat with a single hull.

Outhaul — The line that adjusts the horizontal tension on the main sail.

Pitch-Pulling — When the bow of a catamaran dips below the surface.

Point of sail — A sailing direction with specific trimming requirements.

Port Tack — When the wind blows over the port (left) side of the boat.

Port — Left as a sailor faces forward towards the bow.

Reach — The direction or point of sail 90 degrees from the wind source.

Real Wind — The true, natural wind. As opposed to created or apparent wind.

Rigging — Setting up a boat, making ready for sail.

Rudder — The turning blade in the water, at the stern, attached to the tiller.

Run — The direction or point of sail 180 degrees from the wind source.

Sail — Come on!

Sheet — The line used to control the sail.

Shrouds — The wire mast supports attached to the sides of the boat.

Sloop — A sailboat with a jib and mainsail.

Starboard — Right as a sailor faces forward towards the bow.

Starboard Tack — When the wind blows over the starboard (right) side.

Stern — The back of the boat.

Tacking — Turning into the wind on an upwind course by pushing the tiller away or towards the sail(s).

Telltails — The strips of fabric attached to sails/shrouds indicating wind direction.

The Code — The baffling, convoluted language/customs of the sailing culture.

Tiller — The steering handle attached to the rudder.

Trampoline — The stretched canvas platform upon which sailors sit on catamarans.

Trimming — Adjusting sail tension by pulling in or letting out the sheets.

Upwind — A direction against the wind, towards the wind source.

Wind Circle/Pie — The circular (pie-shaped!) diagram universally used to explain/display the points of sail.

Windward — Situated or moving towards the wind source.

RESOURCES

Sailing centers, dealers, rental outlets, schools, and stores are places to meet people who know about sailing. Look in the yellow pages under boats or boating. Since the first thing your going to do is get instruction and/or rent, your best bet is probably a rental outlet that provides lessons. Folks at these places are also used to dealing with neophytes like you and answering your inane questions is just part of their job. Or should be, anyway. There you should be able to accumulate local information about:

> Sailing Areas
> Sailing Instruction
> Sailing Conditions

> Sailing Museums
> Sailing Organizations

Of course, these dockside operations will also provide:

> Sailboats
> Sailing Gear

> Sailing Literature
> Sailors to talk to

SAILING MAGAZINES

Here are three big ones. There are a few more national publications and every region has some of their own. There is no shortage of reading material on sailing.

Sail Magazine
PO Box 56397
Boulder, CO 80321
800-745-7245

Sailing Magazine
PO Box 249
Port Washington, WI 53074
(414) 284-3494

Sailing World
PO Box 3213
Harlan, IA 51537
800-876-3971

SAILING BOOKS

Chances are your local library will have plenty of books about sailing. After all, it is an ancient activity.

Many sailing stores/outlets/centers will have a book section. Some are absolutely overwhelming. There are thousands of books about every aspect of sailing: boats, technique, navigation, safety, gear, weather, places to sail, rules, cooking, construction, knots, history, you name it. Sailing is just one of those romantic lifestyle pursuits that people like to read and write about. Big time.

Here are three 'bibles' of sailing. Each is a motherload of information:

> *The Annapolis Book of Seamanship* by John Rousmaniere (Simon and Schuster).

> *Royce's Sailing Illustrated* by Patrick M. Royce (Royce Publications).

> *Chapman Piloting, Seamanship and Small Boat Handling* by Elbert S. Maloney (Hearst Marine Books).

TELEVISION

Who can forget ESPN's coverage of the America's Cup off Freemantle, Australia in 1987? The world's most famous sailing competition. Sailing came into the living rooms of millions of viewers worldwide. In America the races became an especially important issue because our team had lost for the first time ever in 1983. The competition became something of a crusade. When Dennis Conners finally won the Cup, it was like V-J Day. The fact that it was Conners who had lost in 1983 made the story even more epic. Like a Hollywood movie. Which of course it more or less became (with an embellishment or two) in the production of **Wind** (See Movies).

Outside of the scintillating plot, ESPN's brilliant camera work really brought the viewers into the boats and the races themselves.

It was probably the greatest promotion for sailing in history. It's a cinch that future America's Cup Competitions will most certainly benefit and become very popular television spectacles henceforth.

The Cup only happens once every few years, but thanks to the wonderful world of cable, other sailing events are periodically aired. Check your listings.

VIDEOS

There are a few videos to choose from. A couple of good ones for beginners are:

Learn to Sail, with Steve Colgate (Bennet Marine Video).

The United States Power Squadron's Boating Course for Power and Sail, with the United States Coast Guard (Hearst Marine Books). This one comes with a book.

John Rousmaniere has a series of videos a tad more advanced entitled *The Annapolis Book of Seamanship Video Series* (Creative Programming, Inc.). They include:

Volume 1: *Cruising Under Sail*

Volume 2: *Heavy Weather Sailing*

Volume 3: *Safety at Sea*

Volume 4: *Sailboat Navigation*

Volume 5: *Daysailers, Sailing and Racing*

MOVIES

The most recent one I can think of that really is all about sailing (or Hollywood's idea of sailing, anyway) is *Wind*, with Matthew Modine and Jennifer Grey (Columbia Tristar, 1992). Outside of the love story, it's about a sailor's quest to win the America's Cup after helping to lose it previously. There are lots of exciting sailing shots and an earnest attempt to convey the passion and competitive spirit of elite sailors.

SAILING ORGANIZATIONS

➤ **US Sailing**
Box 209
Newport, RI 02840
(401) 849-5200

➤ **American Sailing Association**
13922 Marquesas Way
Marina Del Ray, CA 90292

➤ **The United States Coast Guard**
National Headquarters
Washington, DC 20593

➤ **The United States Coast Guard Auxiliary**

➤ **The United States Power Squadrons**

BIBLIOGRAPHY

Alexander, Stuart. *Sail of the Century*. Dobbs Ferry, New York: Sheridan House, 1987.

Johnson, Peter. *The Guinness Guide to Sailing*. Middlesex, England: Guinness Superlatives Ltd., 1981.

Laing, Alexander. *Seafaring America*. New York, New York: American Heritage Publishing Co., Inc., 1974.

Morton, A. Harry. *The Wind Commands*. Middletown, Connecticut: Wesleyan University Press, 1975.

SPECIAL THANKS

Craig McClain— The guy who took the shots is one of the leading photographers in Southern California and is gaining national recognition for his computer graphics as well. An avid sportsman, Craig shreds (shreds?) in golf, tennis, and skiing. Yes. He knows how to sail.

Mission Bay Sportcenter— I couldn't have done it without 'cha. Cliff Graves, Connie Max, and Tom Heasley are the expert instructors/models in all the shots. They and the boats they sailed were provided by The Mission Bay Sportcenter, San Diego, California— one of Southern California's premier rental/instruction/sales centers for wind and water sport. Moreover, owner/operators Rich and Dee Gleason provided much needed advice, editorial comment and encouragement as the project unfolded.

The MBSC facility is renowned for its ideal location, impressive array of boats and equipment, and seasoned, professional staff. You simply won't find a better crew anywhere. For further information call (619) 488-1004.

Fast Lane Sailing Center— It was owner/operators Ron and Debbie Lane who came up with the idea for this book in the foist place. Besides that, they and their fine staff supplied photos, technical assistance, and their enthusiastic support throughout.

Fast Lane is easily San Diego's largest small sailboat dealer. Ideally located next to Seaworld on Mission Bay, they offer one of the widest selections of popular small craft in Southern California. Call (619) 222-0766

INDEX

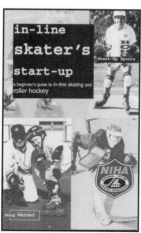

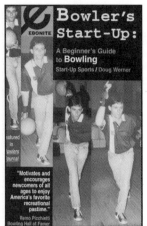

Start-Up Sports

Bowler's Start-Up
Doug Werner
Endorsed by Remo Picchietti, member of ABC Bowling Hall of Fame.
112 pages.
Over 70 photos.
$9.95
ISBN 1-884654-05-3

Longboarder's Start-Up
Doug Werner
Endorsed by Bill Stewart, celebrated surfer, surfboard designer & manufacturer.
160 pages.
Over 150 photos.
$9.95
ISBN 1-884654-06-1

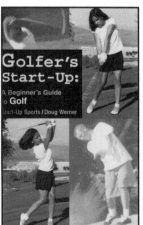

Golfer's Start-Up
Doug Werner
Featured in Golf Magazine. *Includes a journal of the author's learning experiences. Fun & informative.*
160 pages.
Over 100 photos.
$9.95
ISBN 1-884654-07-X

MOre Start-upSports
————→

About the Author

Doug Werner is the author of the internationally acclaimed *Start-Up Sports Series* which includes: *Surfer's, Snowboarder's, Sailor's, In-Line Skater's, Bowler's, Longboarder's, Golfer's and Fencer's Start-Up.*

In previous lifetimes he graduated with a Fine Arts Degree from Cal State Long Beach, built an ad agency and founded a graphics firm.

In 1994 he established Tracks Publishing. Werner lives with his wife Kathleen in San Diego, California: One of the major Sport Funzones of the planet.